Memories of
BOLTON

Foreword.

Memories of Bolton is a compilation of photographs and interesting facts from the past. But there are many other good local interest books of old pictures, so what makes this one any different? The answer to that question is that this book is intended to rekindle memories from the more recent past. In other words, this is not a *history* book, in the sense that the pictures and captions in *Memories of Bolton* relate to a part of our past that is still *within memory* for a great deal of Boltonians. It will, therefore, be no surprise that the period covered by this book is mainly from the 1930s to the early 1970s.

So whether you were there yourself, or your parents were, the pictures bring to life a part of our past that to many folk will seem like only yesterday.

But memories can only be rekindled if there is a good cross-section of local life in all its forms. Maybe you were a regular at the Tivoli cinema, or walked in Moss Bank Park at Wakes with your mum and dad, or perhaps you followed the Wanderers when they won the FA Cup? You'll find plenty of wonderfully nostalgic pictures on all these subjects within these pages.

Of course, no book of this type would be complete without a selection of pictures covering the changes to the Town Centre, and as well as finding a full section on this you'll also be able to study several aerial pictures of the town (reproduced as a full page so they can be seen clearly) taken during the 40s, 50s and 60s.

All in all, then, there should be something for everyone interested in Bolton, be you nineteen or ninety. Whatever your age, I hope you enjoy *Memories of Bolton*

Mark Smith, Publisher

The Queen inspecting troops, Victoria Square, 1954.

Published in 1996 by:
True North Publishing
Dean Clough
Halifax HX3 5AX Tel. 01422 344344
Repro. by Transgraphic Ltd., Morley
Printed by Joseph Ward ColourPrint,
Dewsbury

a true north
publication

ISBN 1900463 45 8
Copyright: True North Holdings.

£4.99 *nett*

Contents

One	*Leisure*
Two	*Shopping*
Three	*At Work*
Four	*The Wanderers*
Five	*Bird's Eye View*
Six	*The Acdo Story*
Seven	*Changing Town Centre*
Eight	*Outskirts*
Nine	*Disasters*
Ten	*Events*

Deansgate, 1949. Just a few years after the end of the Second World War, shoppers were beginning to return in larger numbers to Bolton's Town Centre.

Acknowledgments

The excellent photographs contained within this book were obtained from several sources, and the publishers would like to express their gratitude to the following: Barry Mills and Kevin Campbell of Bolton Local Studies Library for their help and patience in supplying around 35 old pictures, as well as a good deal of other reference material; Andrew Smith, Les Gent, and Christine Bell of the Bolton Evening News, who have allowed the publication of around 35 excellent pictures from the paper's substantial library; Simon Marland of Bolton Wanderers, who provided the various pictures for the section on the club - Simon also penned the captions for the football pictures, John McGoldrick of Bolton Art Gallery and Museum, who also helped with the provision of pictures from the Museum's collection. Special thanks are also due to Chris Driver who researched most of the captions and brought his great wealth of local knowledge to these pages. The publishers would also like to thank the advertisers in Memories of Bolton, most of which are local, long established businesses and therefore part of the area's history. In particular thanks are due to the sponsor of the book, the Astley Dye and Chemical Co. Limited, better known as Acdo, who together with the other advertisers, have enabled us to keep the price of Memories of Bolton to a relatively modest level.

Roll up, roll up, the circus is in town! Or so it was in May 1964 as this Bradshawgate scene shows. This procession of spectacular circus animals was on the way to the Big Top on Spa Road. Today, the use of animals in circus acts is far less frequent , but this wasn't the case in the sixties when this picture was taken, and the crowd were clearly enjoying the spectacle.   Just visible behind the "Elephant Parade" is James Walsh, jeweller and silversmith with Arthur Morris, tobacconist next to Silverwell Lane.

Today, families take their holidays at different times of year to fit in with their own lifestyle, but in the 1940s and 50s it was very different, with many local firms closing down for the annual Wakes holiday. This 1950s view captures the ever popular Punch and Judy show in Moss Bank Park during the Wakes break. The park's swings, swingboats and roundabouts were also in demand along with the donkey rides provided for years by the Court family. During war time a lot of Boltonians took "holidays at home" and Moss Bank Park, close to that other attraction Barrow Bridge was an ideal place for a carefree day out - as long as the weather was fine!

A busy moment in time is depicted in this picture, taken in 1967 on platform two of Trinity Street Station, probably during Wakes Week holidays when trains queued outside the station as far back as Moses Gate and Bullfield. Trinity Street was the start of many Boltonians' holiday trips. In the late 1950s 166 trains stopped each weekday, bringing workers into the town, with the peak of traffic before 9.00 am. Slowly, with the growth of the private car the traffic declined and the great building and its warehouses were not needed any more so were demolished and a new smaller station built on the Newport Street side but incorporating the old clock tower.

Left: The Ghost Train was doing good business in January 1945 and was, like the Caterpillar, always popular with courting couples. Moor Lane had been the site of the fair since 1929 and was preferable to some of the quagmires it has been sited on such as the grass lawns of Cheadle Square and the site of the present Morrisons Store. Bearing in mind the date it is, perhaps, not surprising to see men in uniform. Just four months after the end of the war that had lasted for six long years, people were understandably in a mood to enjoy themselves. (BEN)

Right: New Year's Eve in 1956 at the corner of Ashburner Street and Blackhorse Street showing the fun fair on what is now Moor Lane bus station which still had trolley buses at this time. The fair had long been held in Victoria Square but after the Bessemer's steel works site had been levelled in 1927 the opportunity to free the square of the congestion caused by the fair by moving it to Moor Lane was taken.

This picture shows a fine helter skelter and hand operated roundabouts with the imposing Bolton Gas works in Gas Street to the background. (BEN)

Right: The Rialto Cinema on the North side of Saint Georges Road some time in the 1930s where the first talking picture seen in Bolton was screened. Long before the popularity of television, cinemas were a central part of family entertainment, as well as providing much welcome newsreel shows - particularly in wartime. Like many others in the town the Rialto closed in the early 1960s, eventually re-opening a short time later as an Asian cinema, before closing again. (BEN)

Left: The old Derby Picture Palace in Derby Street near the junction of Thomas Street, undergoing a " futuristic" art-deco style refit in 1938 when it was renamed the Tivoli. The popular cinema lasted until, like the other twenty two in Bolton, it had to give way to the onslaught of television and the new craze of Bingo. The Tivoli building is still in existence as a Bingo and Social Club with next door the exotically named Critchley's Tivoli Scrap Yard. Today the town has only one cinema. (BEN)

A fine day out in Moss Bank Park on Good Friday, April 1958, although judging by the overcoats, perhaps a little chilly. The tricycle being proudly ridden by the boy in the foreground was a "Gresham Flyer" which had a little boot and a telescopic handle for dad to hold to prevent son going too fast. The park of seventy eight acres was opened quite late as Bolton's Queens Park dates from 1866 whereas Moss Bank only officially became a park in 1922.

Right: Moss Bank Park again, with a charming early 1950s view of families relaxing together on what was probably a bank holiday. In the middle distance a number of prams can be seen, which were of the popular "coachbuilt" type. In those days prams were high quality (and high cost) items, and were built to last. Indeed, the pride that many mums took in buying the best quality pram can almost be compared to the pride people take in their cars today! (BEN)

Left: This picture of Queens Park was actually taken in 1935, and reveals a group of young schoolgirls admiring the display of tulips in the flower beds nearest to Chorley Old Road. A recent excavation here had unearthed lots of early 1900s bottles and clay pipes from the local ash pit collections. It is strange to think that the young girls in this picture will now be in their late sixties.

This almost panoramic photograph was taken from the Town Hall steps in the early 1920s. The Gas Offices can be seen prominent to the left. The number of charabancs and people suggest a very special occasion, almost certainly a trip to the seaside. The ride in the "charas" can't have been too comfortable, with solid rubber tyres and only a canvas hood if it rained. Perhaps this was a good excuse to stop at a pub on the way there, and especially on the way back!

Right: Victoria Square in 1963. In 1820 the area occupied by the cenotaph was the new Market Place and the Commercial Hotel served stall holders and customers together. Despite local protests this fine building was closed in April 1972 and demolished in November. The "No Parking" bollard on the corner of the street was a warning of things to come - with the country's first yellow lines appearing in the same year as this picture was taken.

Left: A busy 1940s day in Deansgate. On the left is Abraham Lincoln's which took over the old Graveson's ironmongers shop which later became the New Day furnishing shop before closing in March, 1982. Next door to what used to be Harry S. Taylor's Jewellers can be seen Boots the Chemist, which moved to the corner with Bridge Street in 1961. Littlewoods had taken over the old Embassy cinema and stayed there until 1967. F W Woolworth's store was extended and rebuilt around 1959. (BEN)

Prestons - Jewellers in Bolton since 1869.

The name of Prestons has long been synonymous throughout the North of England as the leading independent jewellers in the region. But the Prestons that we all know today as a business with branches in many parts of the country began over a century and a quarter ago in Bolton - when watchmaker James Preston opened for business.

Early Years

1869 was the year that James Preston began selling watches and jewellery in Bolton. The town was enjoying the relative prosperity that the industrial revolution and the booming cotton trade had brought. Business prospered and the impressive premises at Deansgate in the centre of Bolton were acquired and developed in 1905.

By the turn of the century, Prestons had already forged a reputation as the most comprehensive and prestigious jewellers outside London, with customers coming to Bolton from many other parts of the country, with word of mouth being the major medium for the business to attract new customers.

In 1911 an event that was to be a major influence on the future direction of Prestons occurred when Gertrude Sheppard, great aunt of the present managing director, Andrew Duckworth, joined Prestons. By 1920, Gertrude Sheppard had acquired a controlling interest in the company and since that time Prestons has been a family run business.

The age of expansion

By the 1950s Prestons had continued to build on their reputation as the premier jewellers outside London. This was also the point in time that Gordon Duckworth took over the reins. Realising that demand was continuing to grow, Gordon Duckworth soon began a phase of expansion which saw Prestons open a branch in Leigh, among others.

Left: The 1968 visit of Queen Elizabeth to the town is captured in this picture.

Below: The use of matchbooks and train tickets for advertising is not such a new idea, as these examples produced decades ago by Prestons prove.

The Leigh branch was an immediate success and Prestons were able to consolidate their position throughout the 1960s, operating from more than one outlet. Gordon Duckworth's son Andrew, joined Prestons in 1972 and shortly after this a new marketing tactic saw Prestons become probably the first jewellery retailer in the country to advertise on television.

Prestons for Purses and Note Wallets

Splendid Morocco Folding Sovereign Purse, with Note Pocket. Just right for your friend at the front. Only 2/-

PRESTON'S DRESS and ENGAGEMENT RINGS

PRESTONS LTD for SECONDHAND TAX FREE DIAMOND RINGS AT KEENEST PRICES JEWELLERS FOR NEARLY A CENTURY

for Presents

1970s to the present day

The decision to use the medium of television for Prestons' advertising was to be a major factor in the company's growth over the following fifteen years. The various advertising campaigns during the seventies and eighties established Prestons as "The Diamond Centre of the North - Prestons of Bolton", and this is the phrase that most people still use to describe the company.

In 1980 Andrew Duckworth became Managing Director of Prestons with Gordon Duckworth becoming Chairman. In recent years Prestons have undertaken a planned expansion that has seen them open branches outside their traditional northern base. They now have outlets in York, Altrincham, Guildford and Windsor, and watch concessions in House of Fraser stores in both Birmingham and Manchester. In March 1994 Prestons acquired Croydons - another independent jeweller with two outlets in Bury St. Edmunds and Ipswich, and more recently Prestons opened their first outlet in Scotland, when their watch concession in Jenners department store, Edinburgh, was opened.

The "family run feel" is strong to this day and Andrew's brother Quentin plays a key role as the Director responsible for sales and marketing. Ian Valentine is the Financial Director. A third brother, Neil, takes an interest, but, not a direct role as he has his own successful business. Looking towards the future the plan is to keep growing but at a rate which enables the company to choose the right store in the right town, and to enable their legendary levels of customer care and market knowledge to be maintained at the levels that Prestons customers have come to expect over the last century and a quarter.

Above and Left: Over the years the interior layout and designs of Prestons flagship store at Bolton has changed considerably. The picture above is how the Gift department looks today, whilst the left hand photograph is a late 1960s view of the same floor as a silver showroom, showing how times have moved on. One thing that hasn't changed at Prestons is the impeccable standards of service, choice and value for money that Prestons offer.

Prestons - a company Bolton can be proud of.

From Small to Very Large

UAP Provincial has had an office in Bolton for over 90 years. Currently with over 190 staff, it is one of the town's largest employers.

The Company was founded in 1903 by Sir James Scott, a wealthy cotton merchant, for the benefit of his two sons and future generations. Although he had no previous experience of insurance, Scott used his contacts within the Lancashire cotton trade and his links with the Bolton community to build a successful business.

The Company began as a very local affair - "A Bolton company run by Bolton men" - and the name Provincial was chosen to suggest local links, maturity and respectability, after the use of the world Bolton was ruled out by the existence of Bolton Mutual, another local insurance company.

As Provincial grew, branch offices were established to make it more convenient for people outside Bolton to do business with the Company. The first branches were opened in Manchester (1905) and London (1908) and by 1938, there was a network of 53 offices throughout the country.

In 1919, Provincial's Head Office moved from Bolton to the rural area of Kendal, close to the Lake District where James Scott had a country home.

Bolton, however, has remained important to the Company throughout its history.

Today UAP Provincial is part of the UAP Group, the second largest insurer in Europe. The office at Bolton is one of 4 Customer Service Centres and 19 Branches throughout the UK, meeting the insurance needs of a range of customers from individuals to very large multi-national companies.

ORDINARY

"FIRE" INSURANCE

DOES NOT
COVER THE COST OF THE
CONSEQUENCES
OF THE FIRE

•

Every business should carry "LOSS OF PROFITS" insurance in addition to the customary FIRE cover

FILL IN THIS FORM AND SEND IT TO THE INSURANCE AGENT FROM WHOM YOU RECEIVED THIS LEAFLET

Please send me without obligation, full details of the Monument Insurance Company's "LOSS OF PROFITS" Insurance covering consequential loss over and above the cost of replacing the physical damage

NAME
ADDRESS
NATURE OF BUSINESS

SEND COMPLETED FORM TO

Above right: Provincial office at 1 Acresfield 1904-1909
Far right: Provincial office 1953
Right: Fire insurance flyer circa 1954

Right: Talk about heavy reading! These three workers were kept busy for some time using purpose built wheelbarrows to transfer the book stock from the old Victoria Square library to the new building on Le Mans Crescent, which had just been completed when this 1938 picture was taken. The new building had a reference library, newspaper and periodicals room, lending library, junior library and two lecture halls with one equipped as a cinema.

Left: A group of telephonists at the new Bolton Police headquarters in June 1939 in the Civic Centre. The occasion was a mock air raid and the telephonists were receiving messages from A.R.P. posts all over the borough and learning how to interpret damage reports. The telephone was still a relatively rare item in the average household, and those that were fortunate to have one would usually have to route their call through the local operator, even to make a local call.

Fisher Raworth, built on a tradition of service for over 180 years

How it began

It is, perhaps, not surprising that the name of Fisher, Raworth & Co. Limited is so well known in the Bolton area, when the sheer longevity of the name is taken into account. In fact, the business began in 1816 when the townships of Great and Little Bolton were separated by the River Croal, with a footbridge being the only physical connection between the two. The founder was a man who was to leave his mark on Bolton in many ways, both as a successful businessman and civic leader. Thomas Walmersley, JP., opened his ironmongers shop in Deansgate near to Market Street. Later on he was to open another Iron warehouse in Crook Street, and alongside his business achievements, he became an alderman of the borough and Mayor between 1869 and 1871. After expanding into the production of iron bars at the Atlas Forge, Mr. Walmersley transferred the Oxford Street ironmongers to his brother, Richard Walmersley, and to his friend, James Fisher. This partnership continued until Richard Walmersley's death in 1898, when James Fisher's son Thomas Henry, joined the business, as did another partner, Clifford Raworth. When James Fisher died in 1911 the business was formed into a Limited Company and the name of Fisher, Raworth and Co Limited came into being, and the name remains to this day.

The War intervenes...

Clifford Raworth's two sons then joined the company and the business continued to develop, until the Second World war intervened in 1939. The two Raworth brothers enlisted in the army in 1939 and served throughout the war. Sadly, Sidney Raworth was killed in 1940, but his brother, Frank Clifford survived and rejoined the business in 1945. He was later to become the company's chairman.

Left: This 1950s picture is of a stall at what was probably an ironmongery exhibition. Many of the famous British brand names on show are still stocked by Fisher Raworth to this day, including Spear and Jackson, Rawlplug and Stanley. Doubtless the quality tools on show are still providing good service in someone's toolbox.

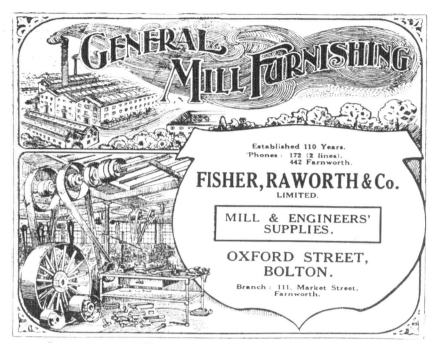

Above: A very ornate pen drawing advertisement from the early 1920s. The three figure telephone numbers give a clue as to how popular that form of communication was at the time.

Right: This poster for the Melitta Coffee Maker was reproduced from a copper printing plate and is thought to date from the mid 1960s. As the wording indicates, this particular item was new to Bolton and interest was thought to be so high that a two day coffee making demonstration was held at the Fisher Raworth's store in the basement of Whiteheads in Deansgate. Many people will remember the store in Deansgate, where a vast choice of hardware was available.

Progress with the times

Right from the early days, the policy of Fisher, Raworth and Co. Limited has been to serve the needs of the industrialist and the householder alike. In the first years of the business there were six blacksmiths working on various projects such as wrought iron gates and railings, with the supply of beam scales being popular amongst local cotton mills.

Later on the business became involved with electrical goods and was a pioneer in the supply and maintenance of such items as vacuum cleaners and televisions sets in the 1940s and 50s. The industrial sector also continued to be a prominent part of the company's activities (and still does to this day) with builders, architects, and the hardware needs of the engineering and textile trade being fully served

Modern Times

In 1943 the stock and goodwill of Entwhistle and Nutter, a 100 year old Bolton firm, were purchased and this led to the acquisition of premises at Spa Road, which is now where the company is situated.

After passing from ownership of the Raworth family, the business is again owned and operated by a family with Bolton links, who also own the Manchester engineering business known as Clare Tooling Systems. Whilst many things have changed over the decades, one thing that remains to this day is the policy of giving the customer the highest possible quality and service, and with 180 years of history this is no idle boast!

Richard Hough Limited Calender Bowl Makers - part of Bolton's industrial heritage.

The Beginning

The history of Richard Hough is an integral part of the history and development of the town of Bolton. Founded in the early 1800s by Richard Hough, the business was initially based on a timber merchants in Nelson Square in the heart of the town centre. Richard Hough then developed his business into the supply of wooden "bowls" with metal shafts to mangle and calender textiles made in the town, (bowl originates from the "bole" of a tree).

Growth and Progress.

Richard Hough's business grew steadily from its humble beginnings and his son, also called Richard, succeeded him. In 1895 large sums were invested in buildings and machinery. After a brief period during the Second World War, when the company was required to produce munitions for the war effort, Richard Hough returned to bowl making and also began to diversify into electric motor armature and stator winding.

Today

Richard Hough, having long since changed into new ownership, moved to a new site at Mill Hill, Bolton, during 1988. There had been no room to expand the original Nelson Square site and wider machines, especially paper machines, meant the need for bigger bowls. The brand new purpose built works includes new 12 metre 3000 ton bowl presses, equal to the largest in the world. The Richard Hough bowl service is supplying 25 countries throughout the world, new innovation coupled with generations of experience.

Richard Hough, founder of the Company that bears his name

Above: Inside the Pressing Rooms of the Nelson Square works, 1905.
Left: An illustration of Calender bowls of 1890, with a grinding machine in the background. One of the bowls displays the 150 inch working-face, tiny compared with face widths today of over 10 metres.

Below: A very well behaved and tidy class at what was previously Haulgh Board School in Elton St off Bury New Road. School Boards were set up by the Education Act of 1870 and children of between five and thirteen were compelled to attend unless they became "half-timers" in a cotton mill at 10 years old and were exempt. In the first year of the Act in Bolton there were 4,000 such children. The First Board School erected in Bolton was Pikes Lane in 1875 and fourteen others were to follow. The Education Act of 1902 made the Town Council responsible for elementary and higher education and from 1903 Board Schools became Council property. This fine school, well over a century old is still standing and used for technical education. The children in this 1940 picture were actually listening to a talk about air raids. (BEN)

Above: Platt Street, 1969. Constructed in the 1880s, Platt Street contained Slater Field Board School and John Holt's weaving shed with Walmsley's vast wrought iron mills at the bottom. At the time this picture was taken residents were complaining of lorries cutting through to Lever Street but would have no complaints with this silent electric Co-op milk float. Bridgeman Street is named after Bishop Bridgeman of Chester who owned land and a country house in Great Lever from 1629. (BEN)

The Wanderers!

Left: Those really were the days for the Wanderers. Captain Nat Lofthouse is cheered by his team mates on the Town Hall steps as he holds the FA Cup aloft, after defeating Manchester United at Wembley in the 1957/58 season.

Right: The 1958 Cup Final side line up on Burnden Park's turf before setting off for what must have seemed a daunting journey to Wembley to face Manchester United. Ralph Gubbins, who had stood in for the injured captain Nat Lofthouse in the semi-final, missed out and was twelfth man.

Pictured standing are: W. Riding, R. Gubbins, D. Hennin, E. Hopkinson, J. Higgins, B. Edwards, T. Banks, G. Taylor, B. Sproston, B. Birch, D. Stevens, N. Lofthouse, R. Parry, D. Holden.

Right: Comedian Ted Loone pays a visit to Burnden Park and is "cup winner" for a day watched by Denis Stevens, John Higgins, Doug Holden, Ray Hartle, Bryan Edwards and Nat Lofthouse, in this 1958 picture.

Below Right: Bolton Wanderers supporters just entering Trinity Street Station for the trip to Maine in March 1953. With their banner proudly held high they were hoping to cheer "the Trotters" on to win the F.A. Cup and just for extra luck they had brought a replica. Football matches were a lot noisier then with home made "rick-racks" and megaphones added to the cheers from even larger crowds (Bolton's official highest gate was 69,912 in 1933). Unfortunately, the Wanderers didn't win that year.

Below: But they did lift the FA Cup in 1958 (and in 1929) and the team that started that momentous season is pictured: Standing: G. Taylor (coach), E. Bell, J. Ball, T. Banks, E. Hopkinson, D. Hennin, B. Edwards, J. Webster, W. Sproston (trainer), Sitting: W. Ridding (manager), T. Allcock, D. Holden, D. Stevens, N. Lofthouse, R. Parry, R. Gubbins, R. Hartle.

Memories of
BOLTON

Left: Burnden Park has seen many happy moments, some of which are captured in the pages of this book, but its darkest hour is depicted in this picture, taken on March 9th 1946 when thirty three people lost their lives on the Embankment during a sixth round F A Cup Tie between the Wanderers and Stoke City.

Right: More recently, this picture captures the triumphant feeling enjoyed by the Wanderers when they won the Second Division championship in 1978. Seen parading the trophy in front of a euphoric Burnden Park crowd are left to right: Roy Greaves, John Ritson, Frank Worthington, Peter Nicholson, Ray Train, Tony Dunne, Peter Thompson and Jim McDonagh.

An aerial view of Burnden Park taken in September 1971, showing the construction of Saint Peter's Way. Bolton Wanderers moved to Burnden Park between 1895 & 1896. The area then was mainly countryside apart from a few small coalmines. The course of the main arterial road into Bolton from the South was arrived at due to the road following the course of the canal that preceded it.

Bolton Town Centre in 1961 looking towards the Town Hall and civic buildings. In the bottom centre is the scaffolding for the new Boots and Halfords stores. Most of the streets in the shot are now traffic free pedestrian zones.

Bolton's impressive Town Hall was opened by the Prince of Wales on June 7th, 1873. The plans for the Town Hall went as far back as 1796 when the Trustees of Great Bolton set aside the site shown here but little progress was made until 1838. Many councillors considered that a lavish Town Hall was inappropriate at the time although some would countenance a very simple design without a clock tower. There was a body of opinion that a tower at a cost of £7,000 was a waste of money.

Over a hundred and twenty years after it was built, the Town Hall still stands out as an impressive piece of architecture, and compares very favourably with many of the modern civic buildings that several other northern towns erected in the redevelopment crazy 1960s.

Taken in April 1949 South West of the Town Hall and Civic Centre this aerial picture provides an excellent view of Flash Street Mills, just visible below the centre. Flash Street Mills were variously Pin Mill, Royal George Mill, Royal Sovereign Mill, which was destroyed by fire in 1818, and Great Moor Street Mills. The mills were all spinners and doublers producing mainly 80/200 weft and twist and were owned from 1788 to the late 1950s by Ormrod, Hardcastle and Company Limited. The site is now a supermarket. Several other mills remain in this shot and many mill chimneys can be seen. The cooling tower at the very top of the picture is that of Back o' th' Bank Power Station. Bolton was an industrial town at the time of this picture, with cotton dominating the town's employment, alongside engineering and other heavy manufacturing. Four years after the war, Bolton was again a real "hive of industry."

Looking South West from the Newport Street shops development in the foreground, this 1966 aerial shot provides evidence of the redevelopment that the town centre began to see in the 1960s, the decade of change for many British towns and cities.

Great Moor Street dominates the view from bottom to top left. The street, like Moor Lane goes back to when the moorlands came very close to the centres of population. In 1792 an Act of Parliment allowed this area to be enclosed and the common land sold or rented to the benefit of the ratepayers.

Noteworthy amongst dozens of others interesting features is Great Moor Street Station, terminus for passengers on the Bolton to Leigh railway in 1828 which was followed by a Bolton-Manchester line almost 50 years later.

The cutting for the railway line appears to form a diagonal swathe through the upper part of this picture.

Opened in 1886, Queens Park is the third largest park in Bolton measuring just over 56 acres. Park Road and Gilnow Road are well shown in the bottom of the shot as is the old bandstand and tiered audience area just above Park Road. In the centre top of this 1964 aerial view is Bolton Infirmary, built in 1913 which became "Royal" in 1931.

The presence of leaves on the trees suggest a summer picture. In the middle distance the blocks of medium rise council flats contrast with the many rows of small Victorian terraced houses, built to house the mill workers of the time but still providing solid dwellings over a century after they were built. Paradoxically, some of the houses and flats built in the "concrete orgy" of the 1960s barely lasted for twenty years.

Other Victorian buildings still with us today include many mills, often now used as office parks or even luxury apartments.

The Acdo Story.

In 1919, not long after the end of the Great War, Harry Pilling was a young office boy in a chemical company based in Bolton.

Even though he was only just out of school, Harry had strong ambitions and saw himself as the main breadwinner for his family, a feeling that was brought on by the fact that Harry had lost his father as a young boy.

And so, at the tender age of sixteen, Harry Pilling decided that the best way to make his fortune was to set up his own business, and that's exactly what he did when he founded the Astley Dye and Chemical Company in 1919 - ACDO was born.

The idea that inspired the young Harry Pilling was based on a "miracle" product to help alleviate the drudgery that the 1920s housewife faced with her weekly wash. In those days washing was a chore dreaded by most housewives, with only a washboard, mangle and ordinary household soap to help ease the burden.

The product that Harry Pilling invented - ACDO, was initially sold in the form of a solid tablet. The essential ingredient of the *Acdo Washing Tablet* was Sodium Perborate, a chemical that Harry Pilling had discovered on a previous trip to Germany. The addition of this ingredient meant that Acdo took all the rubbing and scrubbing out of the wash with its ability to remove stains and add detergency.

Harry Pilling, aged about 22

Above: The picture above shows the Acdo works at Mallison Street in 1928. The process taking place was that of wrapping the Acdo tablets in greaseproof paper, before the Acdo label was applied. When this had been done the tablets were stacked on the ledges in front of the tables shown above, before being taken to the despatch area. The process was very labour intensive, in the days before mechanisation became more commonplace. Amongst the workers shown here were Frank O'Connell (second left), Eddie Collinge (fourth left), who later became works manager, and "Teddy" Williams (second right), who was also later to become works manager.

Sales Innovation.

These days most forward thinking business recognise the importance of image, promotions and marketing. But in the 1920s this wasn't always the case. Bearing this in mind the young Harry Pilling's ability to use innovative ways of selling Acdo was impressive, especially from one so young and inexperienced in the world of business. Several aspects of the way that Acdo was promoted bear witness to this: Initially, the solid Acdo tablet needed to be grated into the water, so free graters were offered to housewives who sent in Acdo wrappers. Harry Pilling also firmly believed in taking the message of Acdo straight to where the buyers were likely to be. To this end he organised free demonstrations in local church and school halls, inviting the local housewives to come along and bring their washing, offering free teas to those who attended Bolton housewives came along in their hundreds, to witness Harry's mother washing their clothes with Acdo

Right: This display of Acdo packs would have been taken at one of the demonstrations held by Harry Pilling and his mother. The posters proclaim Acdo as the "twenty minute washer."
Bolton housewives attended these demonstrations in their hundreds.

Left: Promoting the benefits of Acdo to the Grocery trade has always been an important task, and this 1934 Exhibition Stand is evidence of this.

and hear Harry's sales talk. The result was that sales grew strongly, with word of mouth spreading about the time saving "miracle" washing product.

Early Days.

After starting his business in 1919, Harry Pilling and his mother initially produced the washing tablets in their kitchen. Using a mixing bowl and spoon, the soap was blended before being rolled out and cut into squares before drying. It was then wrapped in greaseproof paper and labelled. Gradually, the success of Harry's demonstrations and other sales tactics meant that the popularity of Acdo grew, with local housewives buying it themselves and telling their friends. Eventually, production became so high that the business outgrew Harry's mother's kitchen and new premises were acquired at Mallison Street near Astley Bridge. By 1928, demand was so high that a night shift had to be added.

The pricing policy of Acdo in the early years was based on Harry Pilling's common sense approach to the finances of the business. The 3d price for an Acdo tablet was arrived at, to quote Harry Pilling, in the following way: "a penny to make, a penny to distribute, and a penny for me!"

Progress

The 1930s were a time of progress for Acdo and in 1938 "Shredded Acdo" was launched when the familiar three ounce solid pack was discontinued and a bigger pack introduced containing the same weight of "suet-like" particles. It was now possible to use Acdo straight from the pack, thus make the grater superfluous.

The Age of Television

The growing popularity of television in the mid to late 1950s prompted Harry Pilling to experiment with TV advertising. Yet again his knack for knowing how to promote his product was valuable in recognising the potential that broadcasting the Acdo message into household could have. Success was immediate and sales of Acdo doubled between 1959 and 1962.

By this time Harry's son, Marshall, had joined the company and, working his way up from the factory floor, he became Managing Director in 1956.

Glo White

The second "household name" brand to come from Acdo was Glo White, which was introduced in 1957. This very quickly achieved sales success as a product used to whiten nylons when added to the wash.

Left: Works outings from the Acdo factory were often to Blackpool, as in this 1940s picture. Working at Acdo has always run in the family, with many staff spending their entire working lives there.

Above: Harry Pilling is shown in the late 1950s, taking a close interest in the production process. This picture shows how mechanisation had taken the place of some of the tasks that were done by hand in the early days. Even though Acdo and Glo White are now international brands, the company is still family owned, and Harry Pilling continued to be involved in the business until his death at the age of 83.

As far back as the early 1920s, Acdo was a pioneer of using advertising and sales promotion techniques. These three pictures show how the company carefully used different types of advertising over the years.

Right: This horse drawn "A" board would have been used to publicise the Acdo demonstrations, which were initially run by Harry Pilling and his mother.

Bottom Right: Another very clever promotional idea was the free grater offer which early 1920s housewives could obtain on by collecting Acdo wrappers.

Below: Prior to the popularity of television, roadside poster sites were one of the main ways of advertising. This Acdo advertisement hoarding would have been a common sight around the streets of Bolton, and indeed many other towns throughout the country, in the early 1950s.

And so the success story continues....

The mid-seventies saw ACDO expand its product range in order to meet the demand for a wider range of products and to satisfy the constantly increasing needs of the consumer.

Glo White Net Curtain Whitener soon established itself as a household name and the Glo White range quickly demonstrated the innovative approach to development that was a hallmark of its early years.

Later, the introduction of revolutionary porous sachets, resembling giant tea bags, heralded Glo White In Wash Stain Remover which was soon followed by its tea bag technology stable-mate, Glo White In Wash Superwhitener. These convenient, no mess products soon caught the imagination of the public in the same way that the ACDO soap block did seventy years previously.

The comprehensive Glo White range currently consists of eleven products, including Ultra Wash Booster, Rescue Colour Run Remover, Travel Wash, Wonderbar, In Wash Net Curtain Whitener and Glo White In Wash Colour Catcher, many of which are shipped around the world making it a truly international brand.

With exports to over ten countries world wide, the revolution that started on a kitchen table in Bolton has converts all over the world from Europe, across to the Middle east, down the pacific rim and into Australia.

The 1990s also saw the launch of ACDO Superwash and, in 1996, Original ACDO, both concentrated machine-wash powders. Original ACDO, the latest addition to the range brings the product full-circle, relying on the traditional values and unique benefits of ACDO vegetable-oil soap-based washing powders that have remained so strong for so long.

Like all ACDO soap powder products, these are biodegradable, not tested on animals and are made with over 60% pure vegetable-oil soap.

Company values

The third generation of the Pilling family now controls the dynamic, fast growing business with two of Marshall Pilling's four children directly involved.

Brandon Pilling became Managing Director in 1992, successfully steering the Company along a demanding, strategic path of growth through new product development and by nurturing markets at home and overseas to broaden the potential for even greater achievement.

Younger brother David Pilling is the Company's Operations Director, tackling the complex business of coordinating packaging, production and distribution to make sure that the range of ACDO and Glo White products meet the high quality, performance and service standards customers have come to rely upon.

As a company, ACDO has always been based in Bolton. For many years it has been a major employer in the area with examples of many employees spending their entire working lives with the business, sometimes including several members of the same family.

ACDO is committed to a future in Bolton and to retaining the excellent standing it has earned within the community - a community it has served and supported for over three quarters of a century.

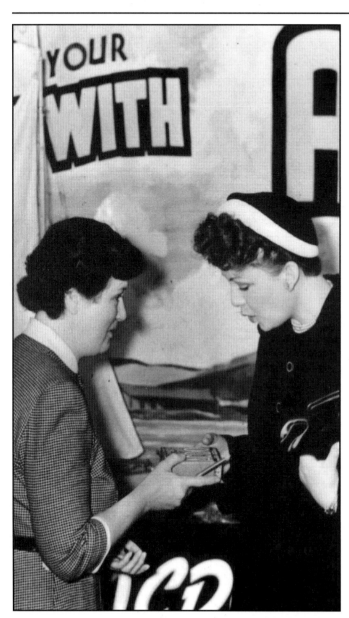

Above: Mrs Maude Pilling, wife of the founder, Harry Pilling is seen here at an exhibition with the actress, Jean Kent, extolling the virtues of using Acdo.

Harry Pilling, founder of Acdo, in his 80s.

Right: Deansgate at its junction with Mealhouse Lane, circa 1958. Dunn & Co. hatters were situated on this site for almost forty years before moving to part of the old Marks & Spencer premises in 1967 which freed the whole frontage for the new Marks & Spencer store.

To the right of Dunn's was George Munro & Co. Bay Horse, better known as "Scotch Vaults". To the extreme right can be seen the Lower Nag's Head so called to distinguish it from the Higher Nag's Head on Deansgate which was between Market Street and Oxford Street until 1930. The original Lower Nag's Head was demolished in the classically inspired three storey Magees of December 1927 which was closed in 1989 to become part of Abbey National.

Left: Looking North towards Flax mill chimney which was demolished in 1972 with the rest of the mill buildings knocked down to make way for the new Bark Street redevelopment in 1985. In the far distance can be seen the ornate cupola of what was the Bridge Street Co-operative Drapery Store opened on Saturday, 30th July, 1897 and destroyed by fire in 1902. It was rebuilt in similar terra cotta style and opened in 1904. To the left is the side of the Imperial Playhouse, closed 1947, with Frank Howard's tobacconists on the same side further down. To the right is F. W. Woolworth & Co which took over Constantines outfitters - Woolies advert outside proclaims the firm's policy for many years: "nothing over 6d." Just to the left of the tram "D" from Dunstar was the old Fish Market, demolished in 1932/33, the only remnants of which were the subterranean toilets soon to close in an economy drive.

A slum clearance picture taken July 1930 after the eradication of "sub standard" property at the North end of Spring Gardens looking across Howell Croft towards Victoria Square. This is a good shot of the Town Hall before it was extended and the Crescent constructed. It is a popular misconception that the Town Hall and Civic Centre date from Victorian times. It makes an interesting exercise to try to see where the old stone of 1873 meets the new. Many slums had to be removed from Spring Gardens and Ashburner Street, with the demolition work well underway by the date of this photograph. The entire Crescent was officially opened by the Earl of Derby in 1939. The Police Department opened in October 1934, the Public Health Department and Public Library in 1938, and the Museum opened in 1941.

The early stages in the construction of Knowsley House, owned by local store Whiteheads replacing much old property including the Bolton Corporation tram waiting room which, when this picture was taken, may even still be temporarily there behind the man on the bicycle. This was, perhaps, the busiest junction in Bolton and prior to automation the trams had to be switched to their various destinations by a "points boy" with a bar to lever them across. This picture dates from around 1932 and by 1933 the tram letter "S" to Church Road and Elgin Street had been replaced by a motor bus. There must still have been some horse drawn traffic around since there is a *"crossing sweeper"* in the centre of the road - what a job!

Russell & Russell, Bolton's legal pioneers since 1887

Mr William Russell

The firm of Russell and Russell is well known today as a forward looking legal practice with offices in and around Bolton, and as far afield as Chester. But the firm's roots began in 1887, when William Russell started his own practice. William Russell was the son of George Russell, a local timber merchant. After receiving a private education he served as an articled clerk under Mr Pennington, a Bolton solicitor, and then Mr C W Dawson.

After starting his own practice the young William Russell diligently set about building his business and his reputation for fair and sound legal dealings soon saw him attract large clients, including the Bolton Union Permanent Benefit Building Society, which was amongst the pioneers of the Building Society movement.

As well as running his own legal practice, the public spirited William Russell harboured ambitions to contribute towards local affairs, but he was unable to find the time to do this until 1898, when an opportunity arose that was to change his circumstances.

Russell joins Russell..

In 1898 William Russell was joined by his younger brother, Walter Russell, in partnership, thus creating the name of Russell and Russell that has been part of Bolton's legal community ever since.

As well as continuing to see the firm develop as one of the areas leading solicitors, William Russell launched himself into a life of public service, which began with him standing for councillor in the Church Ward, where he was elected without opposition. Soon he was contributing to the Electricity, Library and general Purposes committees, helping to shape the future of the borough at what was a time of great civic progress. In 1922 William Russell became MP for Bolton at the general election, with a majority of 6000.

One aspect of William Russell's generosity and public spirited nature that is not so well known is that he was a generous supporter of local charities, indeed for many years he provided a three weeks' seaside holiday for poor children from the proceeds of money left by the widow of his former employer, Mr. C W Dawson.

Although the firm has since passed out of the Russell family hands, the founding principles he brought to the business are still very much evident, an example of this is the major part that the firm is playing in the restoration of Wood Street, home to the firm's head office.

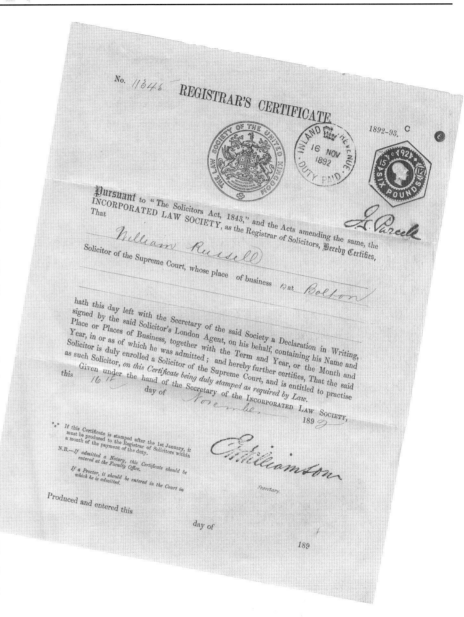

Above: The Registrar's Certificate for William Russell, issued by the Law Society on the 6th November 1892. Six pounds duty was paid, as can be seen from the stamp in the top right hand corner.

Warburton's, a local success story for more than a century.

The story of Warburton's, one of the most respected independent companies in the country, began over a century ago with two brothers, George and Thomas.

Thomas Warburton was not a healthy man. One of a family of ten, he was physically frail and unsuited to heavy manual work. He needed an administrative job. His entrepreneurial brother, George - just back from Australia - offered him a post in his thriving cotton waste business in Bolton. Although he took up the job, Thomas harboured a greater ambition and when a small grocery shop became available in Blackburn Road Thomas asked George to back the venture. He agreed, and in 1870 Thomas and his wife Ellen set up shop. For a time business was good, but after a while the grocery trade slumped. Ellen, who was a good cook, came up with a bright idea. "Let's bake some bread and offer it for sale." Thomas had his doubts, no self respecting Lancashire housewife bought bread - she made her own. But it was worth a try, after all they had little choice. The next day Ellen baked four loaves and six flour cakes and put them in the window....and sold out within the hour. The next day she doubled production and again sold out and within two weeks she was baking full time. The baking side of the business soon began to grow and the shop was renamed "Warburton's the Bakers".

Above: Even in the 1930s Warburton's appreciated the value of well-organised publicity, with music hall star Nellie Wallace tasting the new Eatmore malt loaf, with Henry and his wife Rachel (left) and son George (far right).

Above: Henry and Rachel Warburton with their family.

Whilst things were looking up for Thomas, they were less favourable for George. His cotton business suffered from falling cotton prices and he was forced to close. It was time to review the situation. Thomas was expanding but finding the hours difficult, although George's son, Henry, who had joined Thomas in the bakery, was showing a real flair for the business. The outcome was that George bought the business and the goodwill from Thomas, and decided to develop the baking business with his son, Henry. Henry was to be the real driving force behind Warburton's for the next fifty years, and under his leadership the business grew substantially. After toiling day and night in the original shop, he sold up in 1898 for £989 and bought the Diamond Jubilee bakery in Blackburn Street. At the turn of the century Henry also took on his first full time employee, brother-in-law Walt Pendlebury. He also stood as a Liberal candidate in the North ward of Bolton and was duly elected councillor with a majority of 15 votes. Over the coming years Warburton's was to become the best equipped in the North, but not content with this, Henry Warburton launched his most ambitious project to date - the plan to build his Master Bakery at Back o' th' Bank in Bolton.

Hardly had construction began when Britain went to war. Most of Henry's workforce was called up, including sons Harry and Billy. Undeterred, Henry rolled up his sleeves and aided by his wife, Rachel and daughter Nellie, production continued. In 1915 Rachel Warburton proudly declared the Model Bakery open in front of 500 guests, including the Mayor of Bolton. The end of the war saw Henry's sons return to the business and business move forwards again, although overwork had caused Henry to suffer a stroke in 1918. He was soon at work again, though and in 1920 Henry achieved another ambition when he became a director of his other great passion, Bolton Wanderers Football Club, then heroes of the First Division. The 1930s saw the "Eatmore" loaf launched on the market, with Henry Warburton becoming Mayor of Bolton in 1930. Another great event in the company's history came when George Warburton, inspired by American tastes, dreamt up a new product that was to transform the business, the Malt Loaf. It was an idea that was to sustain

Warburton's until the war. Meanwhile George's brother Billy had made his own impact by developing a retail side, with the first shop opening in 1935 on a new estate in Prestwich. The year after, Henry Warburton died at the age of 71, he was to be missed by both the family and the town. By the mid 1950s the company began to look outside the family for senior personnel, the first time since the appointment of company secretary Jim Aldred in 1936. Expansion continued throughout the sixties with significant acquisitions, including Imperial Bakeries, the manufacturer of Soreen Malt loaf. Between 1951 and 1965 Warburton's grew apace with bread sales doubling and 38 confectionery shops operating alongside the two bakeries. In 1966 another chapter in the history of the company came to a close with the deaths of Harry and Billy Warburton, who had played a key role in guiding the business through the war years and had seen their sons embark on a successful expansion campaign. In the late 1960s the family introduced its Blackpool Milk loaf - an instant hit with children and the elderly and still one of the company's best selling lines. The early 1970s were a period of success with the company seeing continued growth and acquisitions, but by the middle of that decade profit margins were cut to the bone by rising raw materials costs and increased competition. However, Warburton's survived the difficulties by investing in technology and marketing. The 1980s saw the formal establishment of four divisions as well as more acquisitions and expansion into new geographic markets.

Today, Warburton's employs over 2000 people and produces over four million bread products *a day*. Well over a century after Ellen Warburton baked the first Warburton's loaf, Jonathan Warburton, her great, great grandson, can confidently state that "the next 100 years will be even better."

Above and Left: The Eatmore Malt loaf sold well during the 1930s to the late 1950s. Unique, tasty and well kept, it was a favourite of many households, as well as being a testament to Warburton's baking and marketing skills.

Bradshawgate, 1936. Tram letter "O" is just passing Yates's Wine Lodge. The trams had not long to run and many services were replaced by motor buses in 1939. Next to Yates's was Ship Gates which took its name from the Ship Inn which fronted Bradshawgate. In 1890 Yates Brothers Ltd bought the Bulls Head adjoining the Ship Inn and registered it as the fifth of their Wine Lodges in the country. The fine terra cotta building of 1906 still remains. Shipgates as a thoroughfare was closed after a court case in 1975 and Fold Street to the extreme left was closed for the Arndale precinct making it now Bolton's shortest street. Until 1969 it joined Bradshawgate to Acresfield. The gentlemen jauntily walking up Bradshawgate on the extreme right is wearing the standard mens tailoring items of the time, i.e a double-breasted jacket and trilby.

A very similar view to the one opposite, except that this is twenty seven years later. To the extreme left after Yates's Wine Lodge was the well known tobacconist, Frank Howard's with the Fleece Hotel next door and above. The old Fleece Inn was demolished and the road widened with all new buildings in 1907 including the Fleece which in 1972 became the Gaiety and by 1983 with the addition of two shops became Maxim's.

On the opposite side can be seen the Prince William Hotel which in 1963 was a lot taller until the Gallustraole and Cupola were removed in 1971. Further alterations in 1983, 1989 and again in 1996 have led the former old Coaching Inn to become Crompton's Mule. Unusually, there is actually less traffic in the later picture than the earlier, no doubt the photographer waited for a lull!

Bridge Street,1952. The main feature to the right was the Co-operative Society Hall, the venue for many gatherings following weddings, christening and funerals. In 1958 the Co-op supermarket replaced most of this scene. To the right of the Hall was the well known leather goods shop of Crane's established in 1907 at 44, Bridge Street. Flax Mill chimney still dominates the scene and was to do so for another twenty years after this picture was taken. Bolton's town planner and architect wanted the chimney preserved in his plan of 1965 "as a symbol of a new Bolton". (BEN)

Great Moor Street in 1963, taken from the junction of Newport Steet looking east towards Bradshawgate. Further down past the Maudsley Street School was the Turkish Baths, Gregory & Porritts Store and the castellated Salvation Army Citadel known locally as "t 'barracks".

Just visible on the extreme right is Saint Patricks Roman Catholic church opened in 1861 the spire of which became unsafe and was replaced at the centenary in 1961. This picture lends credence to the addage about buses always coming four at once. Like many Bolton Streets, the road surface of Great Moor Street was still made of stone setts when this picture was taken.

Left: Johnson Street footbridge, taken in the early 1960s, looking towards the Town Hall, with its spire visible in the distance.

The bridge was a train spotters paradise but also provided access to Trinity Street Station. Unfortunately for train spotters the bridge was closed in 1980.

Another view of Trinity Street Station, this time in 1935, just before the renovations that were to take place the following year. The bridge was widened late in the 1890s to include what is shown here, a new booking hall, parcels office and cab approach. The canopy remained until 1968, when it was dismantled. The remainder of the station buildings were pulled down in 1987, when the new booking offices opened on the opposite side of the street. (BEN)

Left: Bradshawgate, November 1959, taken from the Balmoral Hotel corner at the junction with Great Moor Street. Most of the property in the centre of the picture which included Wood's pianos and Whittles removals was demolished and replaced in 1963 with Metrolands House. Since 1964 Whittles has occupied larger premises in River Steet and Walton's for Washers has gone as has Marie's hairdressers which was next to the Oddfellows Arms public house.

The Oddfellows was originally owned by Seed's Brewery of Radcliffe but later taken over by Magees who owned most of this block. The pub closed in 1938. (BEN)

Right: Deane Road, April 1953, revealing an experimental and very cheap road junction made out of sand filled oil drums and oil lamps at the very bottom end of Deane Road where it joined Derby Street, Crook Street and Moor Road. Everything shown in this shot has been demolished including the Openshaw Brewery at Number Two Deane Road. It was closed in 1959 and the site would be on a line drawn from the Fire Station across to Walmsley's steam hammer opposite. (BEN)

Above: A slightly overcast Bridge Street in 1958, looking South towards the new Woolworth's store at the top right. Bridge Steet crosses the River Croal close to the site of this shot. Over the years the river has become culverted and more difficult to see. Bridge Street almost became Blackburn Road in 1898 but the proposal was defeated and the Streets Committee left it unchanged. The whole Co-op site is now flattened and ready for redevelopment apart from the old frontage of the banking department on Bow Street.

Two things about this view are noteworthy, compared with life today. Firstly, car parking here was free of charge, and secondly, virtually all of the cars in this car park were British made. The site was that of the first engineering works in Bolton, the Union Foundry of Rothwell and Hick. The huge works of Bessemers Ltd manufactured steel on this site which they also shared with the warehouses and railway sheds at the terminus of the Bolton and Leigh railway. By 1927 the vast area was cleared and by 1930 Moor Lane bus station was operating on part of the site joined shortly afterwards by the Ashburner Street Market. The Odeon building still remains, although not as a cinema anymore. (BEN)

This early 1960s view of Newport Street shows it in its pre-pedestrianised form. At first glance this picture appears to be more recent, but a closer look at the vehicles provides proof of its age. The Ford Thames van parked outside the Derwent Television shop is carrying an advertising message encouraging Boltonians to rent their T.V. The event that had been the catalyst in making television universally popular occurred a decade earlier than this picture, when millions of Britons first watched a national constitutional event, the coronation of Queen Elizabeth. By the early 1960s the local papers were full of adverts for T.V. rental ,with demand boosted by the "new" enhanced picture quality available on the "625 lines" broadcasts.

Victoria Square, 1965. Now called "The Precinct" but 180 years ago the area seen here had a bowling green, an orchard and a meadow with a small stream running through. In 1820 the local market was transferred here from the congested Churchgate. To mark the occasion a wonderful gas lamp of a design by Benjamin Hick was installed. Later Ben's son embellished the lamp with a circular horse trough and a public water fountain. These fine examples of local cast iron were removed in 1925 so that they did not detract from the projected War Memorial. The lamp and trough were never seen again but the drinking fountain was removed to Queen's Park and is still there.

Left: Bradshawgate, 1971. A wintry November day looking South down as far as Nelson Square showing the bright lights of the Arndale Centre. This picture was taken from one of Preston's upper floors of the fine terra cotta building which also contained the firm of Whiteheads. Not many people know that the golden ball on top of the clock tower is a "time ball". Made and erected in 1914 it was hoisted to the top each day at 9.00a.m and at a signal from Greenwich at 10 a.m dropped 10 feet so that local people who could see it could set the time.

Below: Another Bradshawgate view, this time the West side looking North from the Pack Horse almost down to Deansgate and dating before 1969 when most of the premises down to Fold Street closed to make way for the Arndale Centre which opened in September 1971. This area was rebuilt during road widening between 1900 and 1910 and developed again with the Bradshawgate Arcade seen here next to Stone Dri (later the Direct Raincoat Co.) in 1936 which closed complete with all its popular little shops in 1969.

Right: The Bolton Waterworks Committee inspecting work on the new Jumbles reservoir in April 1969 which flooded both sides of the Bradshaw Brook valley from Horrobin Fold to Walsh Fold creating the Jumbles Country Park. The Jumbles was a beauty spot to rival Barrow Bridge for a day out. (BEN)

Left: The construction of the 250 foot high cooling tower in 1936 at Kearsley Power Station in steel and concrete is captured in this picture. Built without the help of modern tower cranes, the cooling tower was the highest of its kind in the world.

On the site once stood Kearsley Hall off Hulme Road built by William Hulme but in this century owned by Colonel Starkie. The name survives in Kearsley Hall Road. The tower and four others were spectacularly blown up in May 1985 and the site is now a housing estate. (BEN)

Left: A Bolton Corporation double decker bus, Number Four to Barrow Bridge, taking a difficult corner at the junction of Mount Street and Pen Street in Halliwell. Due to the difficulty in rounding the corner Bolton Highways Committee was in the process of acquiring the land to remove the corner. Mount Street is much shorter now due to the new Brownlow Way built in 1950. Many workers at Barlow and Jones mills nearby lived here and many more used the old Number Four service from Townleys Hospital through town and on to Barrow Bridge. (BEN)

Right: Oh dear, roadworks were again causing problems on Blackburn Road in Astley Bridge. Looking down towards the Tippings Arms and Tippings Road in this 1953 picture, the cause of the trouble was a fifteen foot hole that "appeared" in the road. The hole was caused by the main sewer, culvert and covered drain from Astley Brook to the sewage works area down Tippings Road. This main sewer shown on maps as early as 1882 collapsed, taking with it all the sub and top soil followed by three inches of tarmac. The chaos this would cause today is unimaginable and was followed by another, much more serious sewer collapse at Fylde Street four years after this picture was taken.

Right: On October 12th 1941 two 500 kilo high explosive bombs fell in the area occupied by Punch Street and Ardwick Street, near to the bottom of Deane Road. Tragically, eleven people were killed by the blast and sixty four others were injured.

The factory of Bolton Heald & Co Ltd was totally destroyed as was part of Joshua Crook Ltd on Deane Road. Eighty houses were rendered unsafe, some of which were half a mile away.

The first attack on Bolton in the Second World War was on January 9th, 1941 when a single bomb fell at the corner of Crook Street and Burns Street and destroyed four houses and "Jimmy's Cafe". The last attack was in April 1942 when 18 bombs and incendiaries fell on the lower part of Smithills Dean.

The Emergency Food Van in the main picture was one of a number provided free by Henry Ford and his son Edsel. This one was maintained at no cost by Gordons of Bolton.

Above: The devastation caused by the bomb raid is graphically portrayed in these two pictures. One can only imagine how these people coped with a disaster on this scale.

The four pictures on this and the facing page are all taken around Fylde Street on the 13th of September 1957. This was the day after what would become known as the Fylde Street Disaster had occurred. At ten past seven on the morning of the twelfth, following prolonged heavy rain, a small hole was seen in Fylde Street, just east of the junction with Hall Street. Concerned residents contacted the Police. Soon afterwards ground movement was felt in the area and the hole began to enlarge. By dusk on that day a crater had grown the length of Fylde Street, some 120 feet long, 18 feet deep and 20 feet wide. (BEN)

Nineteen houses were damaged beyond repair and had to be demolished. Miraculously, the timely evacuation of over a hundred houses prevented any serious casualties and the Mayor's distress fund was later to raise £5,000. This money was shared between seventy three Bolton and fifty seven Farnworth families (Fylde Street was on the border between the two towns). The Victorian sewers that had collapsed, causing the crater to appear, were rebuilt between 1959 and 1961 at a cost of £1 million. At the time the story made the headlines not only in this country but as far away as America.

Events

This August 1939 picture of Bolton Artillery soldiers marching up Trinity Street in readiness for war is likely to evoke both sad and proud memories for readers who were alive during that most difficult period of twentieth century history. It is difficlt not to look at this picture of proud soldiers and wonder how many of them lost their lives in the six years of hard fighting that was to follow. Founded in May, 1860 as The Bolton and Great Lever Volunteer Artillery, they were the first artillery volunteers to see action during World War One when they met a force of Germans and Turks on the Suez Canal. All of the property shown to the rear of the troops in this picture was destroyed in a £1 million blaze in March 1981.

In contrast to the picture opposite, this happy scene is from August 1945, celebrating VE Day and the end of the War. One of hundreds of street parties across the country, this was in Furness Avenue, Tonge Moor. Most of these childrens' fathers would probably still be away at war or engaged in war work. During the course of the Second World War, over 1,500 people from Bolton and district lost their lives, many of those from the Royal North Lancs Regiment who recruited locally. Bolton suffered relatively little by comparison with nearby cities and official records state " only" a total of five tons of high explosive bombs fell on the area between 1939 and 1945. (BEN)

May 1943 was the official start of the "Wings for Victory" appeal week, intended to raise funds for more British military aircraft and launched by Colonel Oliver Stanley, Secretary of State for the Colonies. This busy scene in front of the Town Hall was the Ceremonial Parade and March Past Salute taken by Air Vice Marshall Victor Tait. The aircraft was a Hudson and to mark the opening there should have been a fly-past of mosquito fighter bombers but for some reason they concentrated their aerial display over Lostock, much to the delight of the residents there. (BEN)

Victoria Square, 1954. Several hundred people took part in the Service of Remembrance of 1954 on what is now the Town Hall traffic-free precinct. The memorial was unveiled in July, 1928 by the Earl of Derby and incorporated two existing groups of statuary placed together in position on the memorial. The sculptor was Walter Marsolen, M.C. and the group on the left symbolises "Struggle" whilst that on the right shows "Sacrifice" with "Peace". Prominent behind the memorial in this view was Northern House ladies fashions; Thomas Cook & Son, travel agents; Duckworth's, lingerie; Ye Olde Toffee Shoppe; Ribble Motor Services and just about visible, Alstons grocers. (BEN)

Happy crowds await the Queen

Just over a year after her coronation, Queen Elizabeth visited Bolton to the delight of the towns residents. Despite the wet weather, both sides of Deansgate were packed like sardines, as this elevated view shows. It is a popular Bolton legend that a member of the Royal Family will not pass within sight of the market cross in Churchgate. It usually goes on to explain that on Wednesday, October the 15th, 1651, on the site of the present Market Cross of 1909 the execution of the leader of the Lancashire Royalist, the Earl of Derby took place. The Queen appeared not to heed this legend.

Right and below right: Summer parades and processions, usually held by local church groups at Easter, have taken place for generations. These two pictures show one such parade running through Victoria Square in the mid 1960s. There were substantial crowds alongside the parade, with many spectators taking advantage of the Town Hall steps as a make-do "grandstand". Can you recognise any of the faces in the crowd? (BEN)

Below: Another photograph of the Queen's visit to Bolton of October 1954. The Queen is seen here inspecting the Royal North Lancs Regiment in the centre of Victoria Square. Thomas Cook travel agents are still to be found in the same location today. (BEN)

Richard Threlfall - a great man from a great age

On the last day of 1910 a serious fire destroyed many of the original buildings of the Richard Threlfall Group, together with many historic records. The history of textile engineering as well as that of the company is the poorer for this loss. The meagre material that remains, however shows Richard Threlfall to have been a pioneer in an age noted for its great men.

His ability and energy contributed much to the establishment of Lancashire's cotton industry. His particular achievement was a fine spinning mule and later developments of it were based on his early work.

He improved and developed its 'drawing-out' or carriage gear, ratching, drawing up and copping motions. The Threlfall mule was noted for spinning medium and fine yarn. From 1880 the firm concentrated on it. Entries in Mr Threlfall's notebooks show he had a keen interest in the smallest details of his work. Because his two sons, Richard and Fred had died as young men., the business was carried on by executors and trustees after Mr Threlfall's death until, in 1883, his son-in-law, William Hurst became the proprietor. Mr Hurst too invented several major improvements and was a worthy successor. He had entered the firm as a fitter-apprentice and worked his way up in preparation for taking over.

Once in charge he spent most of his waking hours at the factory. His health was not good and he died, after a brief illness, in January 1906, at the age of 47. He was succeeded by his widow and his son, Mr Richard Robert Augustus Hurst. Known to both friends and business associates as 'Gus', deferred to his father's opinion that an apprenticeship with the firm would be more use to him than a university degree. At the Bridgeman Place Works he served in every department which varied experience served him well when it was his turn to take over the company. In 1910 came a disastrous fire. All employees had been given a half day holiday, it being New Year's Eve. £10,000 worth of damage was done.

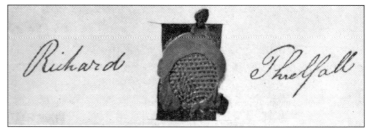

Fortunately the firm was covered by the Provincial Insurance Company but 250 men were thrown out of work.

Gus took the opportunity to have a complete reconstruction and modernisation. No sooner was the firm back on its feet than war broke out and it was set to making bombs, shells and fuses.

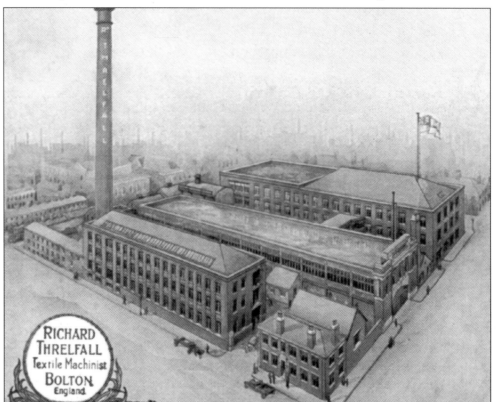

Above: *The signature of the first Richard Threlfall taken from a deed of 1835.*
Left: *An early portrait of William Hurst, the company's second chairman.*
Left: *Bridgeman Place Works in 1934.*

Gus's wife, Margaret bore him two daughters and then twins who died in infancy. In 1918 a long-awaited son was born, Richard Threlfall Hurst.

At work modern machines and central heating was installed. The last Threlfall mule was sold in 1932, though after sales maintenance was continued. The company continued to make ring spinning frames. During the second war Threlfalls made shell cases, rockets and various aircraft components. The depleted workforce was helped out by 250 women workers who were trained and supervised by Gus, who had been requested by the government to serve his country by remaining with his firm. Gus's son, generally known as Dickie, did benefit from a university education, reading for a BSc in Technology at Manchester.

In 1948 the firm became Richard Threlfall Holdings with Dickie and his sisters joining Gus on the board. The firm was still making ring spinning frames for both traditional natural fibres and the new synthetics. Gus died in 1959 in the middle of a cotton decline. Dickie decided to diversify rather than sell up. The firm made ring spinning frames until 1978 but, with a reduced workforce, through acquiring other firms, added to its range of products. They included airport ground equipment and mining equipment in conjunction with Gullick & Dobson.

The company had been experimenting with various types of valves. In 1965 their work was taken up by the Ministry of Defence for use in conventional and nuclear powered submarines and surface vessels.

The valves had the trade name 'Orseal' and they were also useful in chemical plants, in fire-fighting and in the gas industry. They played a vital role in the Falklands Campaign.

Dickie, who had taken a leading role in the commercial and business life of Bolton, retired when he was 65, though he remained as Chairman. His son, Richard junior, also a graduate engineer and his son-in-law David Speak took over the day-to-day running of the business. Towards the end of the recession of the early 1980s, the company started investing in modern technology. Purchasing the first computer and CNC machine tool in 1982, an investment process that continued throughout the decade. Also at this time the business was expanded by the acquisition of the 'Gummers' range of valves, and the development of a range of Ball Valves targeted at Naval and marine applications. This enabled the business to sell to the Off-Shore Oil Industry and to manufacture and supply valves throughout the world.

In 1985 a new venture was started, selling Silicone rubber. This has steadily developed so that today GB Silicone Technology not only supplies liquid Silicone rubber to a wide variety of industries, but also compounds heatcuring rubber, which is used to mould or extrude a multiplicity of products by its customers. This now forms a major part of the company and is steadily growing.

In 1994, the valve-manufacturing part of the business was sold, though the firm continued to use its expertise in that field to buy and sell valves, mainly for companies supplying the Off-Shore Oil industry.

For the last few years Richard junior has been Group Managing Director with David Speak running the 'Orseal Valve' company and Geoff Vickers running 'GB Silicone Technology'. Regrettably in 1996 Dickie hurst died, after being Chairman of the Group for 37 years, in that year Richard junior took over as Chairman.

Threlfalls remains a small firm with the personal touch. The family spirit is typified by the way the company chose to celebrate its 150th anniversary. A Blackpool hotel was completely taken over by the entire workforce. The company hopes to continue to run the silicone rubber and valve sectors of its business as separate concerns. With a proud history to look back on, they are confident of a successful future.

Above left: A single speed mule as made by Threlfalls in 1934.
Above: Richard Threlfall Hurst OBE, Chairman 1959 - 1996.

Over 100 years of good old fashioned service to Bolton's shoppers....

When you walk under this sign, you can be assured of a warm welcome and good service

The name of Gregory and Porritts has been synonymous with quality retailing in Bolton since 1895. An achievement like this is only possible because the company offers an unbeatable package of choice, value and service which has seen it prosper for over a century. So for the best selection of lighting in the region, you know where to look....

Gregory & Porritts Ltd.
14 Great Moor Street
Bolton
Tel. 01204 370044
Fax 01204 521330

The range of lighting on show is enough to satisfy all tastes.

Rigby Taylor - keeping the lawns of Britain beautiful

Herbert Rigby and Robert Stanley Taylor, both of Lytham St Annes, set up Rigby Taylor & Company early in the 1900s. They prospered and soon moved to Victoria Works in Garside Street, Bolton. This site had been a large iron foundry known as Bessemer's Forge. Here the company became Rigby Taylor Limited.

Wigglesworths
Meanwhile, James William Wigglesworth, brother in law of Stanley Taylor, who had previously been in business with him, took over a derelict silk mill in Westhoughton. His company was Wigglesworth Limited and, in the converted silk mill it made pharmaceutical products. The staff, locally recruited, referred to it as 'the pill works'.

Mr Wigglesworth was known for his generosity. He had given the town a conservatory in Queen's Park, a chapel in the grounds of the crematorium at Overdale, a fountain in Victoria Square and a jewel for the Mayor's chain. The town recognised all this by making him a Freeman. Mr Wigglesworth comes into the story again later.

Up to 1934, Rigby Taylor Limited had operated as a drysaltery and manufacturing chemist. The firm made bleaching, dyeing and softening agents for the cotton and woollen trade in Lancashire and Yorkshire. It also produced lubricating oils and soft and liquid soaps for the textile trade and for shampoos.

Its fertilizer Division had been associated since the early thirties with turf products for lawns, golf courses, bowling greens, cricket pitches and general playing fields. The division's most important products were considered to be its Selective Weedkiller and No 2 Moss-killer. It also traded in general garden goods including seeds, containers and tools.

Soon, the company had its own fleet of delivery vehicles in distinctive orange and green. The division had a retail outlet at Victoria Works and also an advisory service for sports clubs.

Above: *The front of an early catalogue from the Fertilizer Division showing the results of using the company's products on flowers, vegetables and turf.*
Left: *An early drawing of the premises at Victoria works in Bolton.*

The company made 'Lysol' and a product known as Mellowite for softening fabrics, There was even a small perfumery.

Before the thirties the paint that the company made was oil-based and only a small range of pigments could be offered. Under Mr Stanley Taylor's guidance, beginning in 1934, cellulose lacquers were developed, including, in 1937, experiments on lacquer for stencil printing on fabrics.

The result was sold to textile printers in Nottingham until the fashion changed and Rigby Taylor went back to producing paints for general purposes which could now be given good gloss and weather-resistance.

During the Second World War the company made blackout and camouflage paints and those for vehicles and aircraft used in the war. After the war there was a return to making polyurethane lacquers, coach and machinery enamels and products for textile screen printing.

In 1953 came the link between Stanley Taylor and his brother in law, James William Wigglesworth. Wigglesworth-Taylor (Holdings) Limited was formed and registered. After Mr Taylor's death, Mr Wigglesworth took over as chairman of Rigby Taylor Limited until his own death a few years later.

As the textile trade declined, less and less of the company's original products were required, so that the Fertilizer Division and Taylor's Cellulose Lacquer Company correspondingly expanded. The latter company became Rigby Taylor Limited (Paints Division), whilst an Automotive Division was set up to cater for the vehicle refinishing trade.

Today Rigby Taylor Ltd are the Number One supplier of Fertilizers, Grass Seeds and Chemicals to the Leisure Industry in the UK. Customers include many of the leading Football, Cricket and Golf Clubs along with Local Authorities nationwide.

Left: An advertisement for Mellowite, produced by Rigby Taylor at Victoria Works. In its favour so the copy says is that it is 'equal to Glycerine. Cheaper than tallow. Helps the Cooking of the Starch or Flour'.

Below: Sports ground turf of exceptional quality benefitting from Rigby Taylor's fertilizer at Messrs Salts (Saltaire) Ltd, West Yorkshire in the 1950s.

Creams Paper Mill - over three centuries of paper manufacturing

Thought to be the second oldest surviving paper making manufacturer in Britain, the Creams Paper Mill, part of Danisco Paper Ltd has operated from the banks of the River Irwell at Little Lever for over three hundred years. Paper was still very much an experimental material when the founder of the company, James Crompton took over a weaving shed on the banks of the Irwell in 1677 to set up one of the first manufacturing plants in the country.

Since those early days, the business has changed hands on seven occasions and the processes involved in the production of the paper products has changed beyond recognition. One thing has remained unchanged, and that is the location of the business, situated as it is, on the original site near the steep wooded valley that forms part of the Nob End Nature Trail.

The area now occupied by Creams Mill has probably been an industrial site of some description for four centuries. Many early records describe how the ownership changed hands in the early years, and how the structure of the firm emerged over time. James Crompton's will, in 1704, referred to 'Higher Mill' which he left to be divided between his two sons, and 'Lower Mill' for which his sons paid an annual rent of just £8, the same amount that James had paid for Creams in 1677. Lower Mill is the Creams of today. Several other paper mills existed in the Little Lever area in the eighteenth century and

it is likely that the Crompton family of papermakers had, at certain times an interest in most of them.

By 1811 Creams Mill was being run jointly by Adam and Joseph Crompton, descendants of the original founder. Sadly the men did not run the business for long, as both were dead by 1812. Joseph Bealey, their nephew inherited the Creams operation and ran it for five years until going bankrupt and dying at the age of 34. William Broadbent acquired it in 1840. Eventually the business was taken over by John Hutchings, and the family turned the fortunes of Creams Mill around over a period of around fifty years.

The Hutchings family owned the business until the outbreak of the Second World War. The mill was closed between 1941 and 1949. A major figure in the relatively recent history of the mill was Joseph Lyddon who is credited with development of the

business in the important post-war period, though the firm was still known as 'Broadbents'. More recent changes in ownership resulted in the change of name to Trinity Paper Mills, in 1968.

Modern times have seen major developments at Creams Mill, making the company one of the region's most historic and successful paper mills, and a common theme throughout has been a concern about the environment.

The area around the mill at Little Lever nestles in a secluded haven nurtured over many years. From the road, the mill cannot be seen or heard, and only as the tree-lined drive sweeps past the administration offices does the full site come into view. The company's concern and commitment for the environment can be traced back over a period of decades.

The visual improvements to the site and the continual drive for efficiency have certainly not been carried out just to meet the requirements of new legislation.

The firm strongly believes in living in harmony with the local environment and its residents. As its mills enter an exciting new era in their illustrious history, that relationship is considered vital for continued success.

In 1992 the company was taken over by Danisco A/S., the huge foods-to-packaging group. Since then the firm has invested millions of pounds in its Lancashire operations. Much of the new plant is designed with the aim of improving quality, rather than increasing total production.

Facing page, bottom left: Creams Mill in 1962. (The Canal Building towards the top of the picture was built in 1955 and destroyed by fire the following year - being restored promptly).

Facing page, top right: "What goes up...!" An explosion in 1980 sent an oil tank crashing through the roof of the mill.

Left: A speech given by Denis Lyddon in September 1963 to mark the official opening of the new offices. With him were the mayor at the time and A.G. Jeans, later Sir Alick.

Below: The modernised premises at Little Lever, Bolton.

Gregory and Porritts, one of Bolton's longest established retailers.

The name Gregory and Porritts is one that generations of Bolton people will be familiar with, not too surprising bearing in mind the fact that the company has had a presence in the town since 1895.

The company was founded by the two local families and traded from Bolton's Market Hall, moving to the Great Moor Street premises in 1925. By the 1940s, approximately sixty outlets in the North West were trading under the Gregory and Porritts banner, including stores in Blackpool, Chorley, Preston and even across the Pennines in Bradford.

The range of goods stocked by Gregory and Porritts was very wide and the prices low, with a "Penny Bazaar" theme.

The business continued to prosper and enjoyed a period of steady growth throughout the immediate post war period.

The ownership of the Porritt family came to a close in the 1970s when they sold the company to local businessmen Fred Bridge and Brian Hayman.

Since that time the emphasis of Gregory and Porritts has switched to that of being a specialist retailer of lighting and furniture goods. As recently as 1994 the original Great Moor Street store was extended into the former Salvation Army premises, where furniture is sold under the banner of Delta House.

Left: This very ornate certificate was presented to Gregory and Porritts as a result of the business exhibiting at the Market Hall Tenants Exhibition of that year. In the four corners are pictured members of the Bolton Corporation Markets Committee. They are: Alderman S. Dickinson (top left); Alderman W H Brown (top right); R. Pike, president of the committee (bottom left) and S. Goodrich, honourary secretary,

Our previous customers are our best salespeople.

A local business you can trust.

WINDOWS...DOORS...CONSERVATORIES...CLADDING...SOFFITS
BARGEBOARDS...GUTTERS...GENERAL BUILDING WORK UNDERTAKEN

Qualified
tradesmen

**WINDOW FIT PLUS
4 PENDLE DRIVE
HORWICH
BL6 7HP
TEL. 01204 693332/840394
MOBILE. 0973 825713**

Guaranteed
work

LEIGH'S PAINTS

LEIGH'S PAINTS - Many well known engineering and construction projects are protected by our range of high performance coatings. Established in Bolton in 1860, Leigh's are now one of the largest private and independent manufacturers of high performance coatings in the U.K. Continuous research and development allied to investment in modern plant and equipment has produced many technical innovations and kept Leigh's at the fore in their market areas.

Technology changes but our traditional values of quality and service remain the same, we give satisfaction to our customers at home or overseas, in construction, industry or commerce. Protection and decoration is afforded to a variety of projects for commercial or government users and chemical, petrochemical and energy installations, protecting even in the most demanding conditions

Quality is not new to us - we were one of the first paint companies to obtain BS.5750 quality assurance for firms of assessed capability and have Ministry of Defence AQAP4 quality approvals and as members of the Demming Society, we are committed to quality improvement.

Quality supported with service. We offer a wide range of expertise for meeting the day to day requirements of our customers - technical advice, ordering and delivery. We provide technical support and cost effective specifications for any project, no matter how small or how complex or exacting.

Leigh's Paints original factory in Flax Place (now the Market Place)

Leigh's Factory and Office today occupying a large site on Kestor Street.

LEIGH'S PAINTS

SUPPLIERS OF A WIDE RANGE OF HIGH PERFORMANCE COATINGS FOR LONG TERM PROTECTION

W. & J. Leigh & Co. Tower Works - Kestor Street - Bolton BL2 2AL - Tel: (01204) 521771 - Fax: (01204) 382115

Cert. No. FM828 SIC 2551

The story of John A Holt Decorators Ltd.

At the end of the last century , in 1899, John Alfred Holt, master painter, started his own business from his end terraced house in Vernon Street, Bolton, employing his father, Abraham, who was also a time served craftsman.

His business profited from regular customers in the Chorley New road and Heaton areas of Bolton, and he was soon able to employ more craftsmen, whose only means of transporting ladders and materials was by pushing a handcart, sometimes as far as Horwich before starting a days work.

During the first world war when all painters were conscripted, John Alfred Holt remained with his father to carry on the business until the cease of the hostilities in 1918.

New Premises

In 1926 the company moved to new premises in Arkwright Street. John's brother, Wilfred was engaged as foreman and later took over the business following John's retirement.

It was in 1930 that a young Albert Todd, nephew to Wilfred, became apprenticed to the business, before joining the Army in the spring of 1940 and the Second World War. Before his return to Bolton, Albert's painting skills were put to good use teaching at the rehabilitation centre in Bedfordshire, after which Albert accepted the offer of a partnership with Wilfred who ultimately retired after 12 months.

New Sole Proprietor

On becoming sole proprietor, Albert moved his family into the premises at Arkwright Street and began the hard task of rebuilding the family business.

Gradually, as the work capacity and the workforce increased the old system of "laying off" during the winter became less frequent - a practice which Albert remembered with hostility.

John A. Holt (Decorators) became a limited company in 1955 and continued to build on it's reputation for quality. Albert's son, Stephen, became apprenticed in 1966.

Following a compulsory purchase order for Arkwright Street in 1963, premises in Astley Bridge were acquired and re-organised to suit the purpose of an enterprising Painting and Decorating company, and in its third home - which was originally the mews to the mill owning Hesketh family - John A. Holt (Decorators) Limited continues to thrive, whilst at the same time retaining its standard of excellence as laid down by its predecessors.

Albert Todd retired from the business in 1982, and died in 1990, his skills and management ability continue through his son Stephen.

Bolton's professional decorators since 1899.

Since 1899, when John Alfred Holt first started our company, we have been proud to serve the needs of domestic and business customers in Bolton. Schools, College and Universities are also amongst our list of satisfied customers.

As well as a business with a long and successful past, we are looking to the future. Determined not to rest on our laurels, our policy is to offer the best service, with qualified tradesmen working to the high standards that our customers, quite rightly, expect.

Above all we provide:

A GUARANTEE OF QUALITY ASSURANCE
A COMMITMENT TO CUSTOMER SATISFACTION
TRADESMEN CONVERSANT WITH ALL DECORATIVE FINISHES.

John A Holt (Decorators) Ltd

Established 1899
 Newnham St., Astley Bridge
Bolton
BL1 8QA
Tel. 01204 594522
Fax. 01204 307263

You'd be amazed at what you can find out about the history of your area!

Moving the stock of books from the old Library to the "new" Central Library was quite a task in 1936.

Finding out about the history of your area is easier than you might think, when you consider the amount of information held in the Local Studies Library. Very accessible in the main Central Library building, the Local Studies Library and Archive Service has access to masses of material on Bolton and the surrounding area. You don't need to make an appointment but do check on the opening hours which are different from those of the main library. The type of material held in the Archives and Local Studies Library includes photographs, maps and plans, parish registers, census returns, oral history on tape, old newspapers, newspaper cuttings, microfiche, newspaper cuttings, indexes of names, places and subjects, archives, books, local government, family and business records, in fact the list is endless. So if you want to find out more about your family history or just the area that you live in , why not pay a visit to the Archives and Local Studies Service.

BOLTON LIBRARY, ARTS AND ARCHIVES - ARCHIVES & LOCAL STUDIES SERVICE.
CENTRAL LIBRARY, CIVIC CENTRE,
LE MANS CRESCENT, BOLTON, BL1 1SE. TEL. (01204) 522311